£2.50
UK only

FLYING START

Treasure Hunting

C.W. Hill

Contents

First published in 1979 by
Sampson Low
Berkshire House, Queen Street,
Maidenhead, Berkshire SL6 1NF

© 1979 Purnell Books Ltd.
SBN 562 00100 X

Designed and produced by
Mallard Publishing
5 Blandford Road
London W4 1DU

Printed by Purnell & Sons Ltd.
Paulton (Bristol) and London

Introduction

One November day in 1807, a farmworker ploughing a field at Tealby, in Lincolnshire, England, turned up a large earthenware pot. Inside it he found almost 6,000 small coins. They proved to be silver pennies minted between 1154 and 1180, during the reign of Henry II. On one side they had the King's portrait and on the other, a cross. Many of them, protected from corrosion by the thick pot, were in excellent condition.

The owner of the land on which the coins were found kept some of them. He gave others to friends, and some went to Sir Joseph Banks, a well-known naturalist and historian. The other coins were presented to the British Museum. Experts there chose about 300 of the best specimens for the Museum collection. The remainder, well over 5,000 coins, were sent to the Royal Mint to be melted down for their silver.

Above: A silver penny of the 1100s minted by Henry II. Nearly 6,000 such coins were found at Tealby, England, in 1807.

Above: This attractive Maiolican pottery dish was made around 1450 in Florence. Crown Copyright Victoria and Albert Museum, London.

Right: Treasures are not always necessarily made of precious metals and gems. This collection mostly consists of 19th century household items.

Above: A treasure hoard in the form of pieces of eight recovered from the Dutch ship Hollandia, wrecked in 1743.

Left: The Tealby hoard was discovered when a farmworker's plough uncovered a pot containing thousands of silver coins.

A similar fate befell some silver coins salvaged not long ago from a Dutch ship wrecked in 1656 off the coast of Western Australia, about 60 miles north of Perth. Bound for Batavia, on the island of Java (now part of Indonesia), the ship was carrying eight chests of silver coins among her cargo. Skin divers rediscovered the wreck by chance in 1963, and treasure hunters later recovered about 7,500 silver coins besides wine jars, ivory tusks and brass candlesticks. Because they were in very poor condition, 2,500 of the coins were afterwards melted down at the Perth Mint.

Although more justified than the destruction of the Tealby pennies, the melting of the Perth coins might have been avoided if they had been discovered a few years later. Many more people now collect coins, and treasure hunting has become an extremely popular hobby. Even if the coins in a newly discovered hoard are not suitable for display in a museum, there are always plenty of collectors happy to buy them. Specimens from a buried hoard or salvaged from a wrecked ship are particularly popular. If treasure hunting had been as widespread in 1807, or even in 1963, as it is today, the Tealby pennies and the Dutch ship's coins might all have been saved from the melting pot.

Not everyone is lucky enough to unearth a pot of silver coins or to salvage pieces of eight from a wrecked ship, but there is plenty of treasure still to be found. Besides coins, millions of badges, buttons, pot lids, bottles, pipes and many other interesting collectors' items are still waiting to be discovered. The purpose of this book is to suggest the best ways and places to search and to describe some of the fascinating bygone items which can still be found.

Famous Finds

Pharaoh's Treasure

In the long history of ancient Egypt the Pharaoh Tutankhamun was not a particularly important ruler. He died in about 1350 BC while still a young man. Like many other pharaohs, Tutankhamun was buried in the Valley of the Kings, in Upper Egypt. The Egyptians believed that, in the next world, a pharaoh would need the furniture, clothing and jewellery he had used during his lifetime. All these, even food and cosmetics, were buried with the body deep underground in a cavern-like tomb in a lonely, desolate spot called the Valley of the Kings.

Over the centuries, robbers looted most of the tombs in the Valley of the Kings. By chance, Tutankhamun's well-concealed tomb was left almost undisturbed for more than 3,000 years. Then, in November 1922, British archaeologists Howard Carter and Lord Carnarvon discovered the tomb. It was crammed with valuable objects, including boxes of jewellery, gold statuettes, a gold-plated throne and a mask of beaten gold portraying Tutankhamun himself. Altogether, the tomb of the young pharaoh contained one of the richest treasures ever found, having over 1,700 items of treasure, superbly worked in gold and precious stones.

Above: A terracotta statuette depicting Pittacus, one of the seven sages of Greece, recovered from the ruins of Pompeii and now in the Pompeii Museum.

Above right: The remains of Pompeii, totally buried by volcanic ash, were one of the world's most exciting archaeological discoveries. Here can be seen part of the colonnade at the north-east end of the forum with the temple of Jupiter on the right.

Left: One of the most famous pieces of treasure, the superbly-worked solid gold mask of Tutankhamun.

Right: Part of the Panagyurishte treasure of ancient Thracian gold, now in the Plovdiv Museum, Bulgaria.

Pompeii and Herculaneum

The treasures in the tomb of Tutankhamun were placed there deliberately. But those found in the Roman towns of Pompeii and Herculaneum were buried in a tragic disaster. The towns lay at the foot of Vesuvius, a volcanic mountain on the Bay of Naples. In AD 79, the volcano suddenly erupted, sending out streams of molten lava and clouds of burning ash which completely covered both towns. Trapped in their houses and shops, thousands of people died within a few moments, suffocated by the ash and dense fumes. When the eruption ceased, the towns had disappeared. During later centuries local builders dug down into the hard ash to obtain stone for new buildings, but it was not until the 1700s that historians suspected that treasure might be found beneath the layers of ash and lava. The classics scholar Johann Winckelmann (1717-1768) was the first serious archaeologist to excavate the site and study the ancient remains.

Since then, archaeologists have excavated almost the whole of Pompeii and much of Herculaneum. Many of the treasures they found are displayed in the National Museum at Naples. These include mosaic pictures and the bronze statuette of a dancing faun.

11

Early Christian Silver

'At first, I thought it was a piece of flint. Then I scraped away the earth and uncovered what I thought was a lead container. Then all these other pieces came out!' In these words, treasure hunter Alan Holmes described how he found a hoard of Roman silver in a field at Water Newton, in February 1975. The hoard consisted of 25 pieces of silverware, among them a wine flask, three chalices, a plate and some thin plaques made in the shape of small palm leaves. From the designs and workmanship, British Museum experts estimated that the silver was made in about AD 300. Latin inscriptions on several of the pieces suggested that they belonged to a group of Christians. Many items bore an early Christian symbol, a monogram formed from the first two letters of Christ's name in Greek. This seems to show that Christians were practising their religion in England long before the Romans left.

Burial Ships

Like the ancient Egyptians, the Anglo-Saxons and Vikings of northern Europe believed that, even after a person died, he would still need the things he had used during his lifetime. A king would need a ship, with clothing, weapons, money, cooking utensils and food for the journey to the next world. The ship might be launched into the sea, burnt on the shore or buried beneath a mound of earth. One such burial ship was discovered in 1939 at Sutton Hoo, in Suffolk, England. The ship's timbers had rotted away, but excavations revealed jewellery, weapons, drinking horns and silverware, some of it beautifully decorated with coloured enamels. A purse of gold coins, mostly minted in France, dated the burial at about AD 625. Archaeologists consider the Sutton Hoo treasure to be the finest yet discovered in Britain. It can be seen in the British Museum, London.

Treasure Island

In 1958, a party of students went to the Shetland Isles to explore the ruined foundations of an old church on St. Ninian's. Near where the chancel had once stood, they came upon a sandstone slab marked with a cross. Beneath it they found a larch-wood box containing an assortment of silverware. It included seven silver bowls, three objects shaped like pepper-pots (possibly ornamental ends of staffs), a spoon and twelve large brooches. One object, part of a sword scabbard, bore an inscription in the language of the Picts, the early inhabitants of Scotland. This, and the style of decoration on the brooches, suggested that the treasure dated from the 800s. The owner probably wanted to hide the treasure from Viking raiders. He was certainly in a hurry, for the objects had been simply thrown into the box. They can now be seen in the National Museum of Antiquities of Scotland, in Edinburgh.

Above: A helmet, one of the many treasures found at the famous Saxon burial mound at Sutton Hoo.

Right: From weapons and other recovered objects we can gain an impression of the life-style of the Vikings.
1 Sword found in Dybeck, Skåne with a gilded silver hilt.
2 Decorated spear heads.
3 Gold spurs of a chieftain from Röd, Ostfold, Norway.
4 Iron axe with a welded edge found in Britain.
5 A Viking brooch found in the Shetland Islands.
6 A seated bronze statuette of the god Thor holding the symbolic hammer.
7 Necklace found in a grave at Birka. Made of amber, glass and bronze.

Treasures from the Sea

The Girona

Names used by Irish fishermen for local headlands led a Belgian treasure hunter to one of the most interesting underwater treasures ever discovered. In 1967, Robert Sténuit was searching for the wreck of a Spanish Armada ship known to have sunk off the coast of County Antrim, in Northern Ireland. Spaniard Rock, Port-na-Spaniagh, and Lacada Point seemed likely places. On the sea bed near Lacada Point, Sténuit found some Spanish pieces of eight, an anchor and a long gold chain. The following year, Sténuit used better equipment and recovered a magnificent treasure now displayed in the Ulster Museum, Belfast. The wreck was that of the *Girona*, an Italian ship that sailed with the Armada. Carrying the crew and valuables of two other ships already wrecked on the Irish coast, the *Girona* sank on October 26, 1588. Among the treasures recovered were over 400 gold coins, nearly 800 silver coins, and many beautiful pieces of jewellery set with precious stones.

The Vasa

Thousands of excited spectators lined the Stockholm quayside on August 10, 1628, to watch a fine new Swedish warship start her maiden voyage. Named the *Vasa*, she was to be the flagship of the Swedish fleet. As she sailed majestically down the harbour, a sudden gust of wind caught the *Vasa* and she began to heel over. Men and heavy tackle slid across the canting decks, water poured into the open gun-ports and, within a few minutes, the great ship had disappeared from sight. Attempts to salvage the *Vasa* began immediately, but all that could be recovered were some of her bronze cannon. The *Vasa* was then almost forgotten until 1956, when Swedish engineers made plans to raise the ship, intact if possible, with all her contents. Their efforts were crowned with success. The *Vasa* can now be seen in a special museum at Stockholm, together with the cannon, coins, cooking utensils, and even clothing and footwear that she carried.

The Association

Modern skin-diving equipment has enabled treasure hunters to explore wrecks that, only a few years ago, would have seemed inaccessible. The Scilly Isles, at the entrance to the English Channel, have been the graveyard of many ships. Three ships: the *Association, Romney* and *Eagle*, were wrecked on the same rocks in October 1707 while making their way home from Gibraltar. The *Association* was the flagship of Admiral Sir Cloudesley Shovell, and carried at least three large chests of treasure belonging to him. Among jagged rocks covered with

Above: The great Spanish Armada, sent by Phillip II of Spain in 1588 to invade England, lost nine or ten ships in battle in the English Channel. At least 50 ships were wrecked while trying to reach home.

Below: 18th century Dutch and Spanish-American coins from the Hollandia.

seaweed and washed by turbulent currents, a team of divers recently salvaged many of the treasures from the ship. They included silver and pewter table-ware, some of it bearing the Admiral's coat-of-arms, and thousands of gold and silver coins.

Treasure Fleet

Most skin-divers would be happy to discover even one wreck with the possibility of treasure on board. Off the coast of Florida, south of Cape Canaveral, lie almost a dozen wrecks. They are Spanish ships sunk by a hurricane in July 1715 while homeward bound with a vast treasure from the Spanish colonies in the Americas. A single ship escaped to report the disaster, and the Spaniards quickly sent an expedition to salvage the treasure. About one-third was eventually recovered, although pirates raided the Spanish shore camps and attacked the salvage ships. After that, the wrecks were forgotten until a local builder, Kip Wagner, found an old Spanish silver coin while beachcombing near his home. This encouraged him to explore further. Since 1961, he has recovered treasure, mainly in gold, worth millions of dollars.

Treasures still to find

Careless King John

Historians have little that is good to say about King John. He is accused of murdering his young nephew, the rightful heir to the English throne, and persecuting that popular hero Robin Hood. He agreed only with the greatest reluctance to Magna Carta, giving ordinary people some safeguard against unjust monarchs. Worst of all, he lost the Crown Jewels.

In 1216, as usual, King John was quarrelling with his barons. Taking a short cut around the wide east-coast inlet known as The Wash, he led his army across a sandy path. During the crossing, a freak high tide overwhelmed the slow, unwieldy baggage carts carrying the royal treasure and swept them into quicksands. For over 700 years, treasure hunters have been seeking the priceless jewels and money-chests that King John lost. Nobody has yet been successful, and the treasure still remains buried somewhere near The Wash.

Pirate Treasure

In 1701, Captain William Kidd, like many other pirates, was brought to Execution Dock, at Wapping, near London, to pay the penalty for his acts of piracy. Before he was hanged, Captain Kidd pleaded for mercy, offering to share with his accusers the vast treasure he had amassed. His bribe was refused and Captain Kidd went to his death without disclosing where his treasure was hidden. Since then, many attempts have been made to locate it. Some treasure hunters believe it to be buried somewhere in the West Indies, possibly in Haiti. Others have suggested Florida or Long Island, New York. Prompted by the discovery of old maps said to have been drawn by Captain Kidd himself, treasure hunters have recently been searching on Oak Island, off Nova Scotia. So far, no trace of Captain Kidd's treasure has been found. Perhaps his offer to share it was no more than a pirate's last piece of bravado.

The Grosvenor

Dipping across the blue waters of the Indian Ocean, rounding the Cape of Good Hope, and heading north through the Atlantic rollers, merchant ships called East Indiamen brought back to Europe the riches of the East. Danish, Dutch, English, French and Swedish ships were among those that made the hazardous voyage with cargoes of silks, spices, ivory, ebony, gold and silver.

On June 13, 1782, the English East India Company's ship *Grosvenor* left Trincomalee, in Ceylon (now Sri Lanka), bound for London. Bad weather made accurate navigation impossible and, on August 4, the *Grosvenor* struck a reef on the desolate

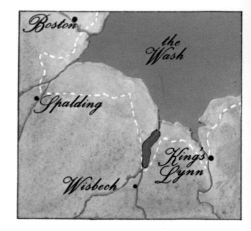

Above: A map of The Wash where the English King John lost his treasure over seven hundred years ago. It is still to be found. The broken line depicts the original coastline.

coast of Pondoland, in Southern Africa. Of the 150 people on board, about 120 managed to reach the shore. Led by the captain, John Coxon, they began a long trek south towards the European settlements in Algoa Bay. But the rigours of the march, shortage of food and water, and the attacks of hostile tribesmen gradually took their toll. On the 91st day of the trek, one of the survivors, a seaman named William Habberley, reached a Dutch farmhouse and told of the wreck.

The tragic story spread rapidly. Soon, rumours were rife that the ship had carried a huge treasure of jewels, gold and silver. In 1789, an expedition found a few scattered coins on the shore where the *Grosvenor* had been wrecked. But later treasure hunters met with little success. Some historians insist that the ship carried no more than a normal cargo of tea, china and general merchandise. Yet the story of the treasure persists. Perhaps underwater treasure hunters will one day reach the wreck and discover the truth about the cargo of the ill-fated *Grosvenor*.

Below: Captain Kidd's lost treasure hoard has become legendary. Some treasure hunters believe it to be located in the West Indies while others think that he chose Florida to hide his fortune.

Treasure Underfoot

Footpath Finds

Many of the most valuable treasure hoards have been discovered in lonely places. These may be the scenes of old battles or the sites of towns or villages, once crowded with people but long since fallen into ruin. Single items, like pieces of jewellery, coins, medallions, buttons and keys, are more likely to be found in busy places. People in a hurry often drop such items on footpaths leading to shops, schools or bus stops. Some objects may be trodden into the soil and lost to sight, but most can be located with a metal detector (see page 28). Coins and other round objects may roll some distance from where they are dropped. So the wise treasure hunter searches not only the path but also the ground at either side. Coins and other small metal objects may roll away into the soft earth at the side of the path. Together with the detector, one will need a trowel and fork and a sharp tool such as a knife or an old screwdriver. Remember to replace tussocks of grass and fill all holes before finally leaving the site.

Paths across fields or through woods usually lead to stiles or gates. These are ideal places to search for small treasures. For people often drop objects when they climb stiles, or open and close gates. But not all treasure found in such places is left accidentally. Years ago, a traveller nearing a strange village might decide to bury his valuables, intending to retrieve them after making sure that the villagers were friendly and honest. By choosing a hiding-place near a stile, gate or easily recognized tree, the traveller could be certain of finding his buried treasure again. If for any reason he failed to return, his treasure might lie undiscovered for many years. Even if it consisted only of a few silver pennies or a couple of gold guineas, the treasure would be well worth finding today.

On the Towpath

Before motor vehicles were invented, goods were often transported by river or canal in horse-drawn barges. The bargees, or members of their families, would drive the horses along a towpath by the water's edge. This is why river and canal banks are good places to search for horse-brasses—the small ornaments used to decorate harnesses. Originally intended as charms to ward off evil spirits, early horse-brasses usually depicted the sun, a star or the crescent moon. Later horse-brasses had a wider range of designs. Some showed the coat-of-arms of the company or family that owned the horses. Others commemorated historic occasions, such as Queen Victoria's Diamond Jubilee in 1897. The Welsh dragon, rosettes for England, Scottish thistles and the lucky shamrock of Ireland were other favourite designs.

Above: Old-established paths across fields or through woods and hills are very good places to look for lost treasures. Be sure to search in the soft earth at the sides of the path where coins and other items may have rolled away.

Right: Horse brasses, used to decorate horses' harness, date back to Roman times. On festive occasions, a working horse may have been adorned with as many as a hundred brasses.

Below: A 12th century 'wavy edge' horse shoe and a 'key hole' horse shoe.

In the Grass

People can easily lose coins and small items of jewellery in parks and fields. Once dropped in the grass, an ear-ring, cuff-link or brooch may be very difficult to find. Newspapers often print advertisements offering rewards for the return of articles lost in local parks or open spaces. Any treasure hunter with a metal detector has a good chance of recovering such lost treasure and claiming the reward. But he must remember that there is no such law as 'Finders, keepers!' Anyone finding lost property should report the find to the police as soon as possible or he may be guilty of stealing. If nobody comes forward to claim the property, or if the rightful owner cannot be traced, the police will eventually return it to the finder.

Treasures from Buildings

Left: 19th century enamel advertising signs are now much sought after by collectors.

Below: Fire marks were metal insurance company signs fixed to the outside of buildings to show which company was insuring the property.

Treasures at Home

Our ancestors were surprisingly careless with their valuables. Almost every day, some kind of treasure is found in an old house being demolished. Besides items of lost property, deliberately concealed valuables may be discovered. Likely places to find hidden treasure in old houses include the spaces below floorboards and above ceiling joists, and below the tiles or stone flags near a fireplace. Under two bricks near the kitchen fireplace of his cottage, a man recently found a tea-cup containing 78 English gold sovereigns and half-sovereigns, all dated between 1824 and 1874.

Safety First

Old buildings standing empty, whether being demolished or not, can be very dangerous places. Even experienced demolition workers sometimes suffer serious injury when walls, floorboards or ceilings give way suddenly. To avoid such dangers, the treasure hunter should observe three simple rules. First, before setting foot on a site or in a building, obtain written permission from the owner. Second, ask the foreman in charge of the site for his advice about where it is safe to search. Last, work in daylight, and with at least one other treasure hunter to help. Anyone who ignores these rules is likely to find trouble, not treasure.

Fire-Marks

Collectors of old metal signs and advertisements may sometimes find examples when buildings are being demolished. Among the most popular are fire-marks. These metal plaques were fixed to the walls of buildings to show that the owners had insured their property against fire. Many of the large insurance

Right: The first British insurance company was formed after the Great Fire of London in 1666. Many of the larger insurance companies had their own fire brigades who dashed to the scene of a blaze. Crown Copyright Science Museum, London.

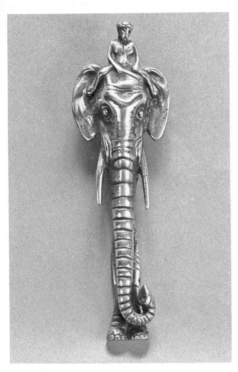

companies used to have their own fire brigades. The fire-mark on the front of a building clearly showed which company had insured it. But there is no truth in the story that, if a company's firemen arrived to find that the burning building was insured by a rival company, they stood idly by while it burnt to the ground!

The fire-marks usually showed the company's emblem. Sun Fire Office fire-marks showed a blazing sun with a human face and the Hibernian Fire Insurance Company used the Irish harp in its fire-marks.

Door Fitments

All kinds of metal objects come to light when buildings are demolished. Even if they are not made of precious metals, they may be interesting and attractive. Before the invention of electric bells, most houses had a brass or cast-iron door-knocker. One favourite design was in the form of a miniature lion's head with a large ring in its mouth. Another popular type was in the shape of a fish or dolphin, joined to the back-plate by its tail so that its head could be used to knock the door.

Other minor treasures found in old houses include ornate letter-box flaps, ornamental door-knobs and decorated finger-plates fastened on doors to protect the paintwork from dirty fingers. Finger-plates were commonly made of porcelain, brass, bronze or cast iron.

Above: An attractive brass door knocker in the shape of an elephant ridden by a mahout.

Digging for Treasure

Local Records

A day too cold or wet for treasure hunting may not be a day wasted. An hour or two spent in the local public library may provide the treasure hunter with information that he can put to good use when the weather improves.

Years ago, most household refuse was tipped into disused quarries, gravel pits, marshes or natural hollows in the ground. After the rubbish had filled the available space, it was usually covered with a thin layer of soil and left for the grass to grow. The sites of such tips may be recorded in town or parish council reports and marked on old maps. By studying these, the treasure hunter may discover long forgotten tips that may yield unsuspected treasures. Local directories may suggest other places to look. They include fields where crowds used to gather, years ago, perhaps to watch cock-fighting or bare-fisted boxing. Other likely locations are the sites of old fords now replaced by bridges, and places where houses once stood. Armed with detailed notes and plans, the treasure hunter will be well prepared for his next search.

trowel

screwdriver

hand fork

sieve

metal rod

string and pegs

Left: Genuine items of treasure such as these have all been found by using a metal detector plus such tools as a trowel, an old screwdriver and a sieve. Don't forget that you will also need a great deal of patience and hard effort!

Right: A good place to search for treasure is the site of entertainments held in days gone by where crowds of people used to gather.

polythene bags

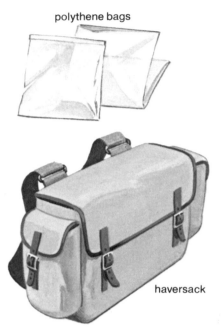

haversack

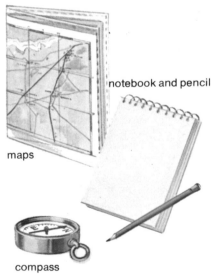

maps

notebook and pencil

compass

Above: Examples of types of basic tools needed for successful treasure hunting. Experienced treasure hunters do much of their searching during winter months so warm, protective clothing is also essential equipment.

Basic Tools

A small, sharp-edged trowel of the kind used in bricklaying is handy for unearthing small objects. Some treasure hunters prefer a screwdriver because its long, narrow blade is easy to push into hard ground. A strong hand-fork is useful for digging in rough, uneven ground. But anyone tackling a rubbish tip will need a garden fork or spade.

Many treasure hunters use a sieve for searching on a sandy beach. Instead of delving down into the loose sand, which quickly swallows small objects, the treasure hunter heaps the sand into his sieve. There he can sift through it carefully before throwing it away and refilling the sieve. Some treasure hunters make their own sieve by drilling rows of small holes in a flat coal shovel. Dry sand runs through the holes, leaving any treasures behind. Other optional tools are a thin metal rod, about 60 cm (2 ft) long, for probing into sand or soft earth, and a horseshoe magnet to pick up small iron or steel objects from dry sand. Methodical treasure hunters often take string and wooden pegs to mark out the area they intend to search. This saves going over the same ground twice.

Repairing the Damage

No matter what tools he uses, the thoughtful treasure hunter makes sure to leave the ground he has searched in the state that he found it. The sea, by washing the sand smooth again, will obliterate traces of treasure hunting below high-water mark on a beach. But a farmer may be justifiably angry to find unsightly holes left in his meadows by people who have been digging for treasure. Some town councils have closed their public parks to treasure hunters because of the damage done to lawns and playing-fields. This could have been avoided if the treasure hunters concerned had carefully replaced every scrap of turf they had lifted, just as cricketers and golfers are expected to do.

23

Rewarding Rubbish

Some of the most interesting finds are made in old rubbish tips. This is because objects once thrown away as worthless may have since become extremely popular with collectors. The thought of digging into a mound of rubbish is enough to daunt the hardiest of treasure hunters. Certainly, a tip used during recent years would be a most unattractive place to dig, and it would be unlikely to yield anything of special value. But a rubbish tip that has not been used for 80 years or more may well contain hidden treasures. With the passing of time, almost all the unpleasant smells will have disappeared. The main danger will be of cuts and scratches from rusty metal or broken bottles. Stout boots and thick gloves are necessary for anyone planning to dig in a rubbish tip, and even the slightest cut must be given proper medical attention. Local records will reveal the whereabouts of hidden tips and rag pits. Remember that permission must be sought before excavations can begin.

Clay Pipes

Almost every old rubbish tip contains some of the small white clay pipes once popular with smokers. Tobacconists often gave the pipes free to regular customers. The pipe makers used wooden moulds, which they carved into fanciful shapes to make the bowls of the pipes more attractive. Some were in the form of a human face or an animal's head. Others had designs with sprays of flowers and clusters of fruit. Hotels sometimes ordered pipes embossed with their names and symbols. The *Crown and Anchor*, the *Bull's Head*, and the *Bunch of Grapes* are typical examples. When clay pipes went out of fashion with smokers, many pipe makers continued to produce them for children to use in blowing soap bubbles. Even if the stem is broken, an old pipe with an unusual design makes an interesting find.

Bottles

Special favourites with collectors are bottles once used for mineral waters. The early types had a rounded base so that they could not stand upright. This prevented the cork from drying and shrinking and allowing the 'fizz' to escape. English bottles of this kind are known as torpedoes, because of their shape, or as Hamiltons, from their inventor, William Hamilton. Another popular type of English bottle is the Codd, introduced about 100 years ago by a Londoner named Hiram Codd. His bottles had a round glass stopper trapped in a pinched neck. The gas from the mineral water forced the stopper against the neck of the bottle, closing it until the bottle was tipped on its side. Codds were still being made during the 1920s and are now popular collectors' items.

24

Right: Durable stoneware bottles are common finds in old rubbish tips. This collection includes bedwarmers, a water feeder for a caged bird and a stoneware water tap.

Centre right: Clay pipes used to be made in a variety of shapes and sizes, some even comical and satirical. They were cheaply produced and plentiful, often being given away with purchases of tobacco.

Below right: Glass bottles. Back row, left to right: mineral water, Edward VII screw neck wine bottle, German disinfectant bottle c. 1890, beehive-topped mineral water c. 1890, Lavender water bottle c. 1910, medicine bottle c. 1900, beer bottle c. 1910. Front row, left to right: 19th century night light, Codd-Hamilton c. 1890, meat extract c. 1920.

Below: A delightful china fairing depicting 'Five O'clock Tea'.

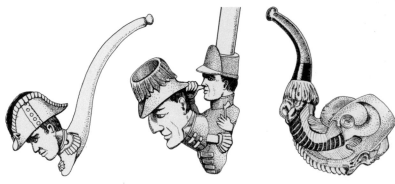

Ornaments

Not every piece of china found in a rubbish tip is cracked or broken. Sometimes a housewife throws away ornaments simply because she is tired of them. And, when people move house, they often discard odd pieces of unwanted china. Typical are the little figures known as fairings, which were given as prizes at fairground side-shows. Roughly made and gaudily coloured, the fairings usually showed humorous scenes, such as a harassed father trying to quieten a howling baby, or a man trying to ride a boneshaker bicycle. Fairings were popular between about 1850 and 1900 and, when they fell out of favour, many were thrown away intact. Today, collectors pay high prices for rare examples. One, showing a lady in a pedal carriage with two top-hatted footmen, was sold for £1,470 at a London auction in the 1970s.

Also popular with collectors are the little china ornaments made by the British firm of Goss and Sons between 1860 and 1940. Intended as holiday souvenirs, the Goss vases, jugs, dishes, miniature plates and other trinkets bore the coat-of-arms of the seaside resort where they were on sale.

Pot Lids

A fortune, it has been said, awaits the person who can discover a simple cure for baldness. One remedy, favoured by gentlemen in the 18th century, was bear's grease. This was made from the fat of bears imported from Russia and America. The melted fat, with added perfume, was then put into small china pots, which were made in Staffordshire, England. At first, the pots bore only the maker's name and a few words of advertisement. But later, some enterprising potters began decorating the lids with black-and-white designs. One firm employed a clever artist named Jesse Austin, who found a way of using transfers to print the pictures on pot lids in several colours. The makers of the bear's grease were delighted because the colourful lids attracted more customers. Many of the pictures showed bears, sometimes behaving like human beings, wearing spectacles to read a newspaper, or studying in a schoolroom. Other pot lids had portraits of famous people, among them Queen Victoria, the French Emperor Napoleon III, the Duke of Wellington and other personalities.

Bear's grease was not the only commodity sold in pots with pictures on their lids. Some of the most attractive designs were on pots of shrimp paste made for sale to holiday-makers by fishermen at Pegwell Bay, in southeast England. The designs included landscapes and pictures of fishermen landing their catch or mending nets. Sometimes the names of the shrimpers were included in the design. These coloured pot lids, called Pegwells, were most popular between about 1840 and 1860. After that, their high cost forced manufacturers, especially of cheap products, to return to black-and-white designs for their

Left: Tiny pieces of Goss china, made as holiday souvenirs bearing the coats-of-arms of seaside resorts.

Below left: The lettering provides decoration and interest on these 19th century pot lids.

Right: Attractive Staffordshire pot lids from fish paste jars. Top: 'Pegwell Bay and Four Shrimpers'. Bottom row: 'Lobster Sauce' and 'The Second Appeal'.

Below: Part of a collection of commemorative mugs. This type of china was cheaply mass produced in large quantities and therefore can frequently be found by the treasure hunter.

pots. Other items sold in decorated pots included cocoa paste and various chemists' products. Many old rubbish tips contain examples of the pots and, more important, their pictorial lids. Collectors are keenly interested in all kinds of old pot lids and are willing to pay high prices for them. Lids with American designs are particularly popular. One, used by a Philadelphia firm, and depicting a buffalo hunt in the Wild West, sold for £450 not long ago. Another, made in Staffordshire and showing a view of the 1853 New York Exhibition, fetched £1,000. These were exceptionally rare specimens, but even ordinary pot lids with attractive pictures and in sound condition are often priced at over £50 each. Anyone who finds two or three lids of that value during an afternoon's digging will have been well repaid for his labours.

A solution of washing soda in lukewarm water is best for cleaning pottery and glass. If the dirt is deeply engrained, the pots and bottles may have to be left soaking. Particularly stubborn stains can sometimes be removed with dilute vinegar or lemon juice. Although they do not corrode as metal does, pottery and glass that have been buried in damp soil for many years do lose some of their quality. Glass, especially, may change colour, becoming opaque and brittle. Collectors refer to this as 'sick glass'. Before trying to clean any fragile objects, the treasure hunter should seek the advice of an expert.

Metal Detectors

A metal detector is an electronic instrument for locating metal objects below ground, behind walls or underwater. A typical model consists of a search head attached to a long handle, and a control box. An audible signal alerts the treasure hunter when the search head is passed near a metal object. In some types of metal detector, the deflection of a needle on a meter gives a visual indication of the presence of nearby metal objects. A detector is a great help for searching open spaces, where small objects can easily slip out of sight in thick grass or under the soil.

Note: In order to operate a metal detector in Britain, a *Pipe Locator/Metal Detector Licence* must be obtained from the Home Office. Any dealer in metal detectors will advise you about this and tell you the address where the necessary licence can be obtained.

Choosing a Metal Detector

There are three basic types:
Beat Frequency Oscillator (BFO) This type is the simplest and cheapest of the detectors. The instrument has two high-frequency oscillators: one with a fixed frequency and the other free-running. When a metal object is located, the free-running frequency alters and the difference between the two is registered on a meter or through headphones.

Induction Balance (IB) The more sophisticated IB has two coils, to transmit and receive, aligned so that the signals are balanced. When the search head locates metal, the balance is disturbed and a signal is produced.

Pulse Induction (PI) The PI has only one coil for both transmitting and receiving. The transmitter switches the current in the coil on and off, causing the coil to act as an electromagnet. Electric currents are produced in nearby metal objects when the current is switched off. Signals from the metal are detected by the same coil.

Cleaning Metal

Having unearthed his finds, the treasure hunter faces the task of cleaning them. Gold is the easiest of materials to clean for, even after being buried for many years, it does not corrode. Warm, soapy water is usually enough to restore its brightness. Silver is more difficult because, in damp conditions, it tarnishes badly. Most other metals corrode too. Soap and water may help, and modern 'dips' are suitable for most silver and brass objects. But old-fashioned metal polishes are too corrosive and will ruin the appearance of a coin. Over the years, bronze and copper may acquire an even coating, usually green or reddish-brown. Known as the *patina*, this coating protects the metal from further corrosion and should not be removed. Indeed, coin dealers charge extra for old coins with an attractive patina. For cleaning metal objects with intricate designs, an electrolysis unit can be used. This runs from mains electricity and will loosen dirt and corrosion. Before trying to clean any potentially valuable metal objects, the treasure hunter should seek advice from an expert at a local museum or an experienced jeweller.

Coins and Tokens

Coins

The most thrilling moment for the treasure hunter comes when he unearths a hoard of coins. Sometimes the discovery of even a single coin can be exciting. A coin found in an English garden in 1976 proved to be a gold aureus minted about AD 290 for the Roman Emperor Carausius, then ruling in Britain. A few months later the finder sold the aureus to a London firm of coin dealers for £8,000. Roman coinage also brought good fortune to a Hungarian farmer's wife. Rummaging among fallen leaves for hazel nuts, she came upon a gold coin. A moment later she found another, and then yet another. Altogether, she unearthed almost 1,400 coins, all of them minted in Constantinople (now Istanbul) during the 5th century AD. The coins went to the National Museum in Budapest and the farmer's wife was well rewarded.

Roman silver denarius depicting the head of Augustus, 27 BC to AD 14.

The Romans provided many countries in Europe and the Middle East with their first stable system of coinage. The large numbers of Roman coins still being discovered clearly shows how widely they circulated. Some of the bronze coins are worth only about £1 each. The silver coins are more expensive, especially in fine condition, and all Roman gold coins are scarce and valuable.

For centuries after the fall of the Roman Empire, most European countries used small silver coins and a few gold coins that poor people seldom saw. As trade and commerce expanded, new coins were needed. By the reign of Queen Elizabeth I, 18 different silver and gold coins were circulating in England. Other countries had almost as many.

Roman copper dupondius depicting Minerva, AD 41-54.

King Charles II introduced the first official English copper farthings and halfpennies in 1672 but the first official copper pennies did not appear until 1797. They were minted by Matthew Boulton, the celebrated Birmingham engineer, and were known as 'cartwheel coins' because the pennies weighed 1 oz (30g). There were also twopenny pieces weighing 2 oz (60g). They had a portrait of King George III on one side and a picture of Britannia on the other. The later pennies were slightly smaller but, in 1860, the copper coins were replaced by bronze coins, which were much smaller and lighter. These were the famous 'bun pennies', so called because Queen Victoria's portrait showed her hair in a 'bun' at the nape of her neck. The coins of Queen Victoria are easy to recognize, but those of 18th century rulers are sometimes difficult to identify. This is partly because many of the monarchs liked to be portrayed as if they were Roman emperors. They wore a wreath of laurel leaves, the symbol of victory, and either an armoured breastplate or a toga, the Roman cloak. The inscriptions on the coins, giving the

Gold Crown of Henry VIII.

Above: The process of minting coins in the 18th century. The two workmen on the left are working the mill or press containing the die for impressing the coins.

names of the monarchs and the countries over which they ruled, were usually in Latin. King William III was entitled 'Gulielmus III Rex' and King Charles IV of Spain became 'Carolus IV Hispaniarum Rex'.

Tokens and Imitation Coins

Even more difficult to identify and value are the many trade tokens and imitation coins that have been issued at various times. Between about 1650 and 1670, and again between 1790 and 1815, England had insufficient low-value coins. Because of the shortage, tradesmen and shopkeepers had serious difficulty in paying their employees and giving change to their customers. To overcome the problem, many tradesmen began to issue their own token coins in copper, brass and silver. Over 10,000 different tokens were issued in Britain and Ireland during the 17th century. The later coin shortage was much more serious, and tokens were issued in even larger numbers. Although sufficient official copper coins were eventually minted, many shopkeepers continued to use metal tokens to advertise their wares. These advertising tokens, and small imitation coins made for use as counters in card-games, often come to light in old buildings and rubbish tips.

Valuation

The value of all old coins and tokens depends mainly on their metal, date and condition. Gold coins are always valuable, but copper and silver coins with bad corrosion or an illegible date are unlikely to be valuable. There are several catalogues of coins and tokens to help the treasure hunter identify his finds. An experienced coin collector or dealer may be able to help in difficult cases.

Badges, Buttons and Buckles

Although coins are the treasure hunter's favourite quarry, a metal detector will lead him to many other small metal objects. These may not have the same cash value as rare old coins, but they often have an interesting story to tell. Tracing the history of a soldier's cap badge or tunic button can be as enjoyable as the discovery.

Badges

Metal badges were introduced in the British Army towards the end of the 18th century. Until then, the soldier's badge was embroidered on his tall cap. If he wore a flat tricorn hat, the badge was simply a cockade of coloured ribbon. When soldiers began to wear stiff leather hats, metal badges were needed. Almost all the early metal badges showed the number by which the regiment was known in the Army list. The number 45 with a crown above it, for example, was the badge of the Sherwood Foresters, who were the 45th Regiment of Foot.

During the 1880s, the British Army was re-organized, and new badges gradually replaced those with the old regimental numbers. Most badges were made of brass or white metal, but those for officers were made of silver. During the Second World War (1939-45), brown plastic was used for many cap badges, but these are now usually made of anodized aluminium.

These various changes may help the treasure hunter to put an approximate date on the badges he finds. A visit to the local library or a regimental museum will often reveal the precise date of such objects and the history of their designs.

Buttons and Buckles

To a soldier, buttons were once almost as important as the cap badge. Many army buttons bore the regimental number or emblem. Early types were made of pewter, but brass buttons were introduced during the 1850s and remained standard for over a century. Anodized aluminium is now used for most army buttons, though some officers' buttons are still made of silver.

Buttons for civilian clothing have been made from so many materials that it is difficult to identify and date them. Bone and ivory buttons used to be popular, but they became expensive. So they were gradually replaced by horn and 'pearl' buttons, the latter made from sea-shells. These, in turn, have given way to buttons made of various plastic materials. The most valuable buttons are those made of gold or silver, and the 18th century porcelain button with painted designs or miniature pictures.

Instead of laces, buttons, straps and buckles used to be the normal means of fastening footwear. In the 18th century, men's shoes were often fastened with silver or steel buckles.

Above: A Wedgwood jasperware button.

Below: Hand-painted porcelain buttons dating from the mid 19th century. The centre button is a Minton design with forget-me-not motif and was made after 1881.

Right: Exquisitely-worked buckles and buttons from the wreck of the Hollandia, *a Dutch treasure ship which sank on her maiden voyage to the East Indies in 1743.*

Above: Intricate detail of gold cape buttons from the Hollandia.

Below: The varied designs of military badges together with their easily traceable histories make these items an interesting subject for a collection.

Medals and Medallions

Medals

A soldier is usually proud of his regimental badge, but even prouder of his medals. Yet so many medals have been awarded to servicemen and women during the last 100 years that some can still be bought very cheaply. Those of the two world wars, 1914-18 and 1939-45, are the commonest, because millions were awarded. The treasure hunter who discovers old medals and cleans them carefully will almost certainly be able to identify them from reference books and catalogues. The ribbons of many medals can be bought from dealers. Renewing the ribbon greatly improves the general appearance of a medal.

War medals were usually made of bronze, brass or silver. Campaign medals often had small clasps or metal bars fixed to the ribbon to denote a particular battle. If these bars are found with the medal, the value is considerably increased as a collectors' item.

Medallions

Matthew Boulton of England was the first manufacturer to use steam-powered machinery for minting coins. The fine quality of his 1797 cartwheel pennies and twopenny pieces prompted other factory-owners to install steam presses. They were soon able to produce small tokens and medallions for only a few pence per 100. As a result, all kinds of local events, celebrations and anniversaries could be commemorated by the issue of cheap medallions. Most were made of copper, brass, bronze or white metal. British city councils presented them by the thousand to schoolchildren to mark Queen Victoria's Diamond Jubilee in 1897. Larger medallions made suitable prizes for success in examinations, sporting achievements and winning displays at exhibitions and trade fairs. Gold and silver medallions were usually carefully preserved, but those in cheaper metals were often discarded when their owners lost interest in the events for which they had been awarded.

If, after cleaning, a medallion is in reasonably good condition, it can usually be identified by its inscriptions. A coat-of-arms can also be a useful clue. The value of a medallion depends on the metal from which it is made, its size, condition, design, workmanship and the importance of the occasion for which it was issued. Collectors prefer bronze rather than lead, brass or copper, and large medallions rather than small. As a general rule, a medallion with the portrait of a celebrity or a coat-of-arms is more valuable than one with only an inscription. One issued for an important occasion, such as a coronation or international exhibition, is generally worth more than one that marked only a local event.

Left: A commemorative medal to celebrate the visit of Napoleon III and Empress Eugenie to London in 1855.

Below left: Commemorative medallions. Left to right: 1886 Colonial and Indian Exhibition, George IV Coronation medallion, 1935 Jubilee medallion.

Below: European military medals relating to World War I are fairly common as there were literally millions issued. Recruitment posters such as this example (right) are also now collectors' items as so few have endured through the years.

At the Water's Edge

Beachcombing

One of the most enjoyable ways to spend a summer afternoon is to go treasure hunting on a sunny beach. A metal detector is a useful aid, as most types work well in fine sand. The movement of the tides is continually dredging small objects from the sea-bed and throwing them up on the beach. There is also the possibility of finding coins, keys, buttons or jewellery dropped by holiday-makers. This kind of treasure hunting is called beachcombing.

The best places to search are those where crowds of people gather, usually near entertainments, below the pier, or near the ice-cream stalls and snack bars. Unfortunately, people sun-bathing or dozing in deckchairs may not welcome the arrival of a purposeful treasure hunter with a metal detector, so the search may sometimes have to be postponed until the beach is less crowded.

Anyone finding a piece of jewellery or a purse containing money should take it to the local police station in case the owner has reported its loss. Modern coins found singly need not be taken to the police, as tracing their owners would be practically impossible.

Beaches on rocky shores where ships have been wrecked are likely places to find pieces of wreckage or coins. This is especially true after stormy weather or exceptionally high tides, which may have disturbed the timbers of sunken ships, releasing small objects trapped in them. Many wrecks containing treasure have been located because a beachcomber found a few old coins tossed up on a beach after a winter gale.

On lonely beaches, or those with rocks or sand-banks, it is best to begin searching about an hour after high water. Move out as the receding tide leaves the beach clear, but take careful note of any channels among the rocks and sand-banks where water remains. The turning tide will fill these more quickly, and might cut you off from the main stretch of sand.

Estuaries, where the current of a river meets the sea tides, can be more dangerous than an open beach, so extra care is essential. Ideal places to search are below neglected quay-sides once used by sailing ships but too small for modern vessels. Sailors were notoriously careless with their coins and trinkets. And, now that so many yachtsmen are using river moorings, there is also the possibility of finding more recent treasures.

Mudlarking

Searching along the muddy foreshore of an estuary is known as mudlarking. When the Thames Embankment was being built in London during the 1860s, mudlarks made a good living from

Above: A sharply-pointed trowel, a small probing tool and even a miner's gold pan are popular treasure-hunting tools.

Below: Beachcombing is an enjoyable pastime for the whole family.

36

the old coins, pottery and other relics that they found in the excavations at the river's edge. Some of the finds dated back to Roman times. But not all the treasures were genuine. Two illiterate labourers, Billy and Charley, found some lead badges worn during the Middle Ages by pilgrims going to the Holy Land. These badges were so eagerly bought by antique-dealers that Billy and Charley decided to make forgeries from scraps of lead. It was several years before archaeologists realized that the badges Billy and Charley were selling were not genuine.

Before starting to search along a river estuary, a treasure hunter should visit the local public library. Maps, trade directories or books on local history will show where old quays, docks or warehouses once stood. Their sites may be excellent places to concentrate on searching.

Avoiding Danger

Treasure hunters on dry land are seldom likely to run into danger, but mud or sand near the water's edge can sometimes be treacherous. Advice from local people who know the estuary and the coastline well may save the treasure hunter some anxious moments. One final word of warning: any metal or plastic object that resembles a bullet, bomb, shell-case or an explosive device of any kind should be left severely alone. Mark the spot where it was found and report it at once to the nearest police station.

Above: Rivers in cities can be most interesting places to search. Sites near bridges can be rewarding as many objects may have been thrown or lost in the river by passers-by. Wide bends where the river flows more slowly are also good sites as objects may be deposited in the silt.

Below: A 'Billy and Charley', a faked copy of a medieval pilgrim badge.

Underwater Exploration

Years ago, exploring wrecked ships was possible only in a deep-sea diving suit. With its large copper helmet and lead weights on feet and shoulders, this cumbersome suit considerably restricted the diver's movements. Its main disadvantage was that air had to be pumped through a pipe to the helmet. Any defect or obstruction in the air pipe would put the diver in great danger. The introduction of the aqualung ended the diver's dependence on help from the surface. It consists of a diving mask, compressed air cylinders and a valve to regulate the pressure and flow of air to the mask. The pioneer of the aqualung was a French naval officer, Commandant Jacques-Yves Cousteau. His invention has given treasure hunters a key to the underwater world. Besides an aqualung, the underwater explorer needs a rubber or neoprene suit for protection against the cold of deep water. Flippers on the diver's feet give him extra swimming power and the popular name of 'frogman'. Other useful equipment include a waterproof watch, a depth gauge, and a strong, sharp knife for cutting away seaweed.

Dense seaweed and viciously sharp rocks hampered the divers who salvaged the treasure of the *Association* in the Scilly Isles. But even more dangerous were the swift and ever-changing currents caused by the ebb and flow of the Atlantic tides around the islands. The divers who explored the wrecks of the Spanish treasure ships off the Florida coast met similar difficulties. They found that visibility was extremely poor on the sea-bed. And, as waves broke over the reefs, the undertow was strong enough to send a diver spinning head over flippers.

Sub-Aqua Clubs

To acquire the skill and experience necessary to overcome underwater hazards, the treasure hunter needs expert instruction. Incompetent use of a metal detector in a sunny meadow may result only in a wasted afternoon. But incompetence on a dark, rock-strewn sea-bed can mean instant disaster. The best safeguard for the budding underwater explorer is to join one of the sub-aqua or skin-diving clubs that have been formed in many large towns. There he will find other beginners to share his problems, and experts who will teach him the basic skills and accompany him on dives. Even when experienced, the underwater treasure hunter should never dive unless accompanied by another club member. Clubs arrange tests of equipment, organize expeditions to likely sites and advise on the cleaning and recording of any treasures that may be brought to the surface. Legal advice may also be needed, for the laws on the salvage of wrecked ships are even more complicated than the laws of treasure trove.

Right: A diver recovering a candlestick from the Dutch East Indiaman Princess Maria *wrecked off the Scilly Isles in 1686.*

Below: The underwater treasure hunter needs the correct equipment in order to dive in safety.

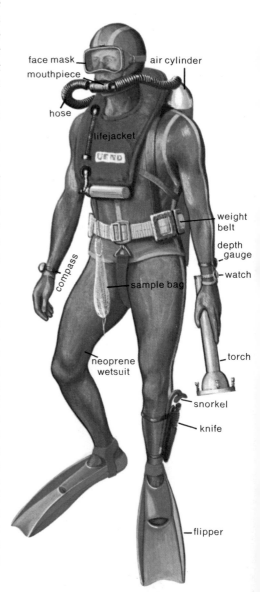

38

Code of Conduct

By adopting this code, the treasure hunter will help himself and others pursuing the hobby. For it is important for all treasure hunters to earn the understanding and co-operation of the people with whom they come into contact.

Code of Conduct

1 Do not interfere with archaeological sites or ancient monuments. Join your local archaeological society if you are interested in ancient history.

2 Do not leave a mess. It is perfectly simple to extract a coin or other small objects buried near the surface of the ground without digging a large hole. Use a sharp trowel or knife to cut a neat circle or three sides of a square, but do not remove the plug of earth entirely from the ground. Extract the object and replace the earth carefully, so that even you have difficulty in finding the spot again.

3 Help keep the countryside tidy, and help yourself. Take any worthless metal objects you dig up to a litter bin. If you ignore this advice, you could find yourself digging them up again next year.

4 Do not trespass. Ask permission from the owner before venturing on to any private land.

5 Report all unusual historical finds to the local museum and seek expert help if you accidentally discover a site that might be of archaeological interest.

6 If you discover any live ammunition or any lethal objects such as unexploded mines, do not touch them. Mark the site clearly and report the find at once to the local police.

7 Learn the laws of treasure trove and report all finds of gold and silver objects to the police. These laws work to your advantage.

8 Respect the countryside. Do not leave gates open, and do not damage crops or frighten animals.

9 Never miss an opportunity to show and explain your metal detector to anyone who asks about it. Be friendly. You could pick up some useful clues to a good site to search. If you meet any other treasure hunters, introduce yourself. You may learn much about the hobby from one another.

10 Remember that, when you are out with your metal detector, you are an ambassador for the treasure hunting fraternity. Do not give us a bad name.

If all treasure hunters were to respect this Code, not only would the pastime become acceptable to archaeologists, but the amateur treasure hunter could also provide valuable information leading to finds of significant historical interest.

Below: Archaeologists at work reconstructing the original earth-brick wall of a royal tomb at Salamis, Cyprus.

Treasure Trove

In Britain, anyone who finds an object made of silver or gold, or containing even the smallest amount of these metals, should report the find to the local police. They will take charge of the object until a legal official, called the coroner, holds an inquiry, known as an inquest. With the help of a jury, the coroner has to decide whether or not the find is to be declared officially as treasure trove. (The word 'trove' comes from the French word *trouvé*, meaning 'found'.)

If the original owner hid the object, intending to return for it later, the coroner is likely to declare it to be treasure trove. But, if the owner lost it by accident, or intentionally threw it away, the coroner will declare that it is lost property. How, the finder may ask, can the coroner and jury possibly make such a decision in cases where the original owner died hundreds of years ago? The answer is that they can only make a guess. If, for example, the find is a single coin or a piece of jewellery, the likelihood is that the owner lost it by accident. But if the find consists of a jar of silver or gold coins, it is likely that the owner intended to return for his money but failed to do so. This might have happened either because he could not find the place again, or because he died suddenly. In cases like this, the find would be treasure trove.

Under British law, treasure trove belongs to the Crown. The coroner passes it to the British Museum, where experts decide whether it should be kept there or, perhaps, in some other museum. If a museum keeps any of the treasure, the finder normally receives a cash payment equal to the full value of the items retained. Objects not required for museum collections are returned to the finder. Strangely, objects that contain no silver or gold cannot be declared to be treasure trove, even if they are of great value or historical importance. Such objects become the property of the finder unless the rightful owner can be found. The same applies to any ordinary items of lost property.

Laws in Other Countries

In Scotland the law of treasure trove extends further than in England and Wales. All Scottish finds of ancient objects, whether of gold, silver or other materials, are treasure trove. They belong to the Crown and must be reported to the police.

After that the Scottish procedure is similar to that in England, except that Edinburgh's National Museum of Antiquities of Scotland has the first claim on any objects it considers to be of historic interest. The rest are returned to the finder or to the owner of the land on which they were discovered.

In other countries, the laws covering buried treasure vary widely. Some countries insist that all finds must be reported to the police, but do not fully recompense the finder for objects that are kept by museums. Other countries allow treasure hunters to keep their finds, but not to export them.

Expert Advice

Any treasure hunter can recognize an old bottle or a pot lid when he finds one. But coins, tokens, medallions and similar small metal objects are sometimes harder to identify, and expert help may be needed. The first place to try is the local library. The Bibliography on page 44 suggests where some of the answers to the treasure hunter's questions may be found. Library catalogues and staff will indicate other books on the same subjects. Another place to seek help is the local museum. Even if members of the staff cannot identify an old coin or token, they will probably know someone who can. And there may be a local numismatic or archaeological society with experts in many fields of knowledge.

Archaeologists are keenly interested in old objects of all kinds. They are always pleased to hear of local discoveries, whether valuable or not. The treasure hunter can help archaeologists by making a careful record of all his finds. Best for this purpose is a notebook listing the date of each find, its exact position in relation to nearby roads, buildings or trees, the depth below the surface, and whether any other objects were noticed. Even a few rusting nails or pieces of rotting wood may tell the archaeologist where an old building once stood and where other discoveries may be made. Like treasure hunting itself, archaeology has become a popular hobby during recent years. The two subjects have much in common, so the treasure hunter should benefit from joining his local archaeological society. But some archaeologists have been upset by treasure hunters taking their metal detectors to historic sites and digging large holes in the turf of ruined castles, abbeys and other ancient buildings. The Code of Conduct on page 40, compiled by a group of retailers of metal detectors, goes a long way towards pacifying those who look unfavourably on treasure hunting.

Above: A 19th century porcelain figure advertising 'Bridal Bouquet Bloom', probably made in central Europe. Crown Copyright Victoria and Albert Museum, London.

Below left: A piece of Roman silver dating from the 4th century, part of a hoard of Christian church silver found in a ploughed field in Britain. By courtesy of the British Museum, London.

Below right: Dutch ceramic tiles made in the late 17th century. The design is painted in manganese on tin glazed earthenware. Crown Copyright Victoria and Albert Museum, London.

Far right: Gold Portuguese coins, English guineas and a sailor's gold poesy ring recovered from the Association, the flagship of Sir Cloudesley Shovell, which sank in 1707 whilst returning from Gibraltar.

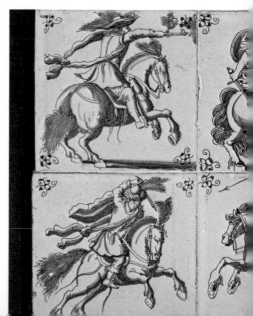

Glossary

Archaeology The study of antiquities, such as ancient sites and buildings, and the objects found in them.

Beachcombing Searching beaches for items of interest, such as lost property, or treasures from sunken ships. Older objects are more likely to be found after strong tides or fierce storms have disturbed the sand or shingle.

Cobalts Bottles made from cobalt-blue glass and used for medicines or poisons. Blue glass was used to distinguish the bottles from those used for harmless liquids.

Commemorative China Chinaware, chiefly mugs, cups, saucers and plates, produced to commemorate important occasions, such as coronations, or in honour of famous people.

Codds Mineral water bottles sealed by a round glass stopper, like a marble, in the pinched neck.

Cumberland Jacks Small brass counters, imitations of sovereigns, inscribed *To Hanover* and issued when the unpopular Duke of Cumberland left Britain to become King of Hanover in 1837.

Doubloons Spanish gold coins or *doblons,* minted from the 14th to the 19th century.

Fairings Cheap, highly-coloured china figures made for sale at fairs or to give as prizes at side-shows.

Goss Ware Small china ornaments made chiefly as holiday souvenirs by W. H. Goss and Sons.

Ground Effect A defect of some metal detectors, whereby slight variations of the distance from the detector-head to the ground causes false signals.

Hall Marks Markings, usually quite small, impressed on objects made from precious metals to show that they have been tested and approved at an assay office as being equal to or better than a certain standard quality. A hall mark also includes symbols to indicate the location of the assay office, the maker or sponsor and the year in which the object was tested.

Hamiltons Mineral water bottles with a rounded base so that they could not stand upright.

Mud-Larking Searching for treasures in the mud of river estuaries and in tidal waters.

Numismatics The study and collection of coins, medals and medallions.

Pegwells Pictorial lids made for the china pots in which fishermen of Pegwell Bay sold their shrimps and fishpaste.

Pieces of Eight Large Spanish silver coins with a face value of 8 *reales.* Also used in the Spanish-American colonies.

Samian Ware Red pottery with a brilliant glaze made in the island of Samos and in many other parts of the Roman Empire.

Sovereigns English gold coins first minted during the reign of King Henry VII.

Spade Guineas British gold coins minted during the reign of King George III, and named after the spade-shaped shield on the reverse. Many brass copies were later made as games counters.

White Metal A cheap alloy containing tin and small parts of copper or zinc. White metal is used mainly for inexpensive medallions and counters.

Bibliography

Buttons for the Collector, Primrose Peacock, David and Charles, 1972.

Buttons, a Collector's Guide, Victor Houart, Souvenir Press, 1977.

Book of Bottle Collecting, Dorothy Beck, Hamlyn, 1973.

Bottle Collecting: Price Guide, Gordon Litherland, Mab Publishing, 1977.

Observer's Book of Glass, Mary and Geoffrey Payton, Frederick Warne and Co., 1976.

Catalogue of the World's Most Popular Coins, Fred Reinfeld and Burton Hobson, Oak Tree Press, 1977.

Coin Year Book, Numismatic Publishing Company, 1978.

Roman Coins and their Values, David R. Sear, Seaby's Numismatic Publications, 1970.

Victorian Fairings and their Values, Lyle Publications, 1975.

Firemarks, John Vince, Shire Press, 1973.

Discovering Hall-Marks on English Silver, John Bly, Shire Press, 1968.

Old Horseshoes, Ivan G. Sparkes, Shire Press, 1975.

Horse Brasses, G. Bernard Hughes, Country Life, 1956.

Commemorative Medals, J. R. S. Whiting, David and Charles, 1972.

Standard Catalogue of British Orders, Decorations and Medals, E. C. Joslin, Spink and Son, 1976.

Orders and Decorations, Alec A. Purves, Hamlyn, 1972.

Collecting Pot Lids, Edward Fletcher, Pitman Publishing, 1975.

Observer's Book of Pottery and Porcelain, Mary and Geoffrey Payton, Frederick Warne and Co., 1973.

Archaeology of Ships, Paul Johnstone, The Bodley Head, 1974.

Tobacco and the Collector, Amoret and Christopher Scott, Max Parrish, 1966.

Digging up Antiques, Edward Fletcher, Pitman Publishing, 1975.

Treasure Hunting, C. W. Hill, Numismatic Publishing Co., 1977.

Index

Acknowledgements

The Publishers would like to express their personal thanks to the following people and organisations for their help and advice: Photographers Philip Carr, Rex Cowan and Roger Johnson; C-Scope Metal Detectors Ltd; Mrs Frith of the Button Queen and Richard Lea of Lost Treasure, Chertsey, owners of the treasure items featured on the cover.

Photo credits
Paul Armiger: 39; British Museum: 12, 42; Philip Carr: 20, 32, 35, 37; Michael Carter: front cover; Rex Cowan: 9, 14 (both), 15 (below), 33 (above and right), 43; C-Scope Metal Detectors Ltd: 2/3, 4/5, 18/19, 22, back cover; Sonia Halliday: 10, 11 (both), 40/1; Mansell Collection: 31; Roger Johnson: 9 (right), 21, 22, 25, 26, 27, 29, 33 (below), 34, 36; National Maritime Museum: 15; Picturepoint: 10, 24/5, 26/7, 30, 34, 34/5; Science Museum: 21; B. A. Seaby: 8; Spectrum: 19; Victoria and Albert Museum: 6, 9, 42, 42/3; Wedgwood: 32.

Illustrators
The illustrations and drawings throughout the book are by Terry Allen Designs Ltd, Richard Eastland, John Fraser, Ruth Hall, Eric Jewel and Jane Roach.